Reference Guide
To the Fidel Phonic Code

American English Edition

Educational Solutions Worldwide Inc.

Copyright © 2009 Educational Solutions Worldwide Inc.
First Edition
Compiled by Educational Solutions with contributions by Dr. Roslyn Young, Malcolm Jussawalla, and Amy Logan
All rights reserved
ISBN 978-0-87825-058-5

Educational Solutions Worldwide Inc.
2nd Floor 99 University Place, New York, N.Y. 10003-4555
www.EducationalSolutions.com

Table of Contents

About This Guide 1
English Language Fidel (Phonic Code Key) 3
Vowel Sounds & Spellings 4
1 buff 5
2 pale yellow 7
3 dark pink 9
4 ice blue 12
5 white 14
6 yellow 16
7 blush 21
8 ochre 23
9 purple 25
10 dark green 26
11 red 28
12 turquoise 31
13 mouse 33
14 pink/mouse 34
15 brown 35
16 white/pink 37
17 ice blue/pink 40
18 brown/aqua 42
19 pink/dark green 45
20 purple/aqua 47
21 ochre/pink 48
22 aqua/purple 48
23 aqua/pale yellow 48

Consonant Sounds & Spellings 50
24 chestnut 51
25 fuchsia 53
26 fuchsia/lime green 55
27 lilac 56
28 yellow/lilac 58
29 lime green 59
30 French blue 62
31 orange 63
32 yellow/orange 64
33 lavender 65
34 yellow/lavender 67
35 mauve 68
36 khaki 70
37 green 72
38 sad pink 74
39 pale lime 75
40 pink 76
41 bright blue 77
42 yellow/bright blue 79
43 pale aqua 80
44 pale blue/aqua 81
45 gold 82
46 light orange 85
47 yellow/light orange 88
48 bottle green 89
49 pale blue 91
50 gray 92
51 sky blue 94

52 dark magenta 96
53 olive 97
54 green/French blue 98
55 gold/aqua 100
56 gold/lime green 100
57 gray/lilac 101
58 gold/sky blue 101
59 gray/French blue 101

About This Guide

This book is a detailed guide to the Fidel (Phonic Code). You may find it useful for planning lessons as well as finding words on the appropriate Word Chart when introducing new sounds and spellings during a lesson.

Each table is organized by the color and column number of the sounds on the Fidel. You'll also find the spellings associated with that sound, sample words, and on which Word Charts each spelling appears (if applicable). The column numbers are assigned on the next page. We recommend you use this guide with the Color Key for the American English Fidel, which is included in your kit.

You may see that some sounds have a (*) beside them. This is to note an alternate pronunciation.

English Language Fidel (Phonic Code Key)

1	2	3	4	5	6	7	8	9	10	11	12	13	15	16	17	18	19	20
a	u	i	y	e	o	a	e	u	o	a	o	e	a	oo	o	I	a	o	u	ou
au	o	o	ey	ea	a	ah	e	o	a	ea	oo	ee	ai	ou	a	i	ai	oe	ew	hou
ai	a	a	ay	a	ho	i	ou	o	au	ah	ew	ea	e	u	au	y	ay	ow	iew	ow
i	ou	u	ee	u	oh	io	oi	i	aw	aa	ou	y	e	o	oa	ie	ey	owe	eau	ough
	oo	e	ai	ai	ow	iou	oa	ea	awe	au	ui	ie	ei	oa	oo	ye	ei	oa	ue	
	oe	ia	ei	ay	eau	eou	eo	ou	ough	e	u	ei	hei	ou	ho	igh	eigh	ou	ieu	**21**
		ie	hi	ie		ia	ai		oa		oe	i	ae	eu	eye	ea	ew	ewe	oi
		ea	hea	eo		ie	ei		augh		ue	eo	aye	ue	ao	eigh	aigh	oh	hu	oy
		ae	ois	ei		au	iu		oo		eu	ey	ayo	oi	is	et	ough	eu	aw
		is		ae		ea	eau		ou		ough	ay	ey		owa	ais	ae	eau	eue
						ah	ough		hau		wo	oe				ei	au	oo	**22**
						he	y		ho		ieu	ae				aye	e	au	oi
									ao			is					ee	eo	
									oi								ot		**23**
									owa										o

24	25	27	29	30	31	33	35	36	37	38	39	40	41	43	45	46	48	49	50	51	52	53	54	55	56
p	t	s	s	s	m	n	f	v	d	th	th	y	l	w	k	r	b	h	g	sh	ch	ng	j	qu	x
pp	tt	ss	ss	z	mm	nn	ff	f	dd	the	the	i	ll	wh	kk	rr	bb	wh	gg	ch	tch	n	g	cqu	xe
pe	te	se	se	ge	me	ne	fe	ve	de		h	j	le	u	ke	re	be		gu	ch	t	ngue	d		cc
ph	ed	's	's	me	mb	kn	ph	ed	t		phth	u	lle	o	ck	wr	bu		gh	s	c	nd	dge		xc
bp	d	z	c	t	lm	gn	gh	ph	ld			'll	c	pb		ckgu	ss	che	ge
tte	zz	ze	ce		gm	pn	lf	've	'd				**44**	rps						sch		gg	**57**
pt	ze	sc		mn	mn	ft		t				**42**	wh	ch	rp				c		dg	x
bp	x	st		'm	gne	ffe		tt				l		lk	rt				sc		dj	
ct	si	sw		in	pph							le		qu	rrh				che			**58**
cht	thes	ps		**32**	on							'll		que	rre				chs			x
th	sth	sce		m	dne									che	lo							
phth	s'	sse			nd									cqu	're							**59**
't		sth			ln									cch								x
	28	z												co	**47**							
26	's			**34**									kh	r								
z				n										re								
zz														're								

Vowel Sounds & Spellings

1	2	3	4	5	6	7	8	9	10	11	12	13	15	16	17	18	19	20
a	u	i	y	e	o	a	e	u	o	a	o	e	a	oo	o	I	a	o	u	ou
au	o	o	ey	ea	a	u	o	e	a	ea	oo	ee	ai	ou	a	i	ai	oe	ew	hou
ai	a	o	ay	a	ho	o	au	ah	ew	ea	ea	ai	u	au	y	ay	ow	iew	ow
i	ou	u	ee	u	oh	i	aw	aa	ou	y	e	u	o	oa	ie	ey	owe	eau	ough
	oo	e	ai	ai	ow	io	awe	au	ui	ie	ei			oo	ye	ei	oa	ue	
	oe	ia	ei	ay	eau	iou	oa	e	u	ie	ei	hei	14	ou	igh	eigh	ou	ieu	21
		ie	hi	ie		eou	eo		oe	i	ae	u	ho	eye	ea	ew	ewe	oi
		ea	hea	eo		ia	ai		ue	eo	aye	eu	ao	eigh	aigh	oh	hu	oy
		ae	ois	ei		ie	ei		eu	ey	ayo	ue	oi	is	et	ough	eu	aw
		is		ae		au	iu		ough	ay	ey		owa	ais	ae	eau	eue	
						ea	eau		wo	oe				ei	au	oo		22
						ah	ough		ieu	ae				aye	e	au		oi
						he	y			is					ee	eo		
							ho											23
							ao									ot		o
							oi											
							owa											

1 – buff: <u>a</u> as in <u>a</u>t

Spelling: <u>a</u>, as in <u>a</u>t

Chart 1	pat, at, tap, apt, as, sat, sap, pass, past, asset
Chart 2	mat, mast, am, stamps, map, Sam, Pam, man, pants, an
Chart 3	fan, fat, dad, mad, and, sad, stand, sand, that, than, yam, path
Chart 4	land, lap, pal, last, add, daddy
Chart 5	ran, rat, after, ask, track
Chart 6	has, hat, back, black, have
Chart 8	thank, bankrupt, hand
Chart 9	cash, match, shall, channel
Chart 10	adjective, act, character
Chart 11	fantastic
Chart 12	photograph
Chart 13	Saturday, family
Chart 14	fast, fasten
Chart 15	anxiety, anxious, exaggerate, examination
Chart 17	calves, half, diaphragm, khaki
Chart 18	hallelujah, pneumatic, champion
Chart 19	accept, language, handkerchief, humanity, ballet, sapphire
Chart 20	guarantee, blackguard, asthma, azure

Spelling: <u>au</u> as in l<u>au</u>gh

Chart 16	laugh

Spelling: <u>ai</u> as in pl<u>ai</u>d

Chart	No words on the charts

Spelling: <u>i</u> as in mer<u>i</u>ngue

Chart   No words on the charts

2 pale yellow: u as in up

Spelling: u as in up

Chart 1	up, putt, us, pup, puppet
Chart 2	must, mumps, pump, sum, nut, sun
Chart 3	fun, stuff, puff, dud, dust, mud
Chart 4	dull, plus, tummy, funny, sunset
Chart 5	run, rust, truck
Chart 6	but
Chart 8	bankrupt, hungry, hundred
Chart 9	shut, much, such
Chart 10	judge
Chart 12	gun
Chart 13	under
Chart 14	dumb
Chart 17	number
Chart 18	budget
Chart 19	cupboard

Spelling: o as in done

Chart 5	love
Chart 6	mother, brother
Chart 8	month, come, done, some
Chart 9	front
Chart 13	money, above, honey
Chart 20	tongue

Spelling: a as in was

Chart 4	was

Spelling: **ou as in young**
   Chart 11   young
   Chart 16   tough

Spelling: **oo as in blood**
   Chart 11   blood

Spelling: **oe as in does**
   Chart 8   does

3 dark pink: i as in it

Spelling: i as in it

Chart 1	pit, it, tip, is, sit, sips
Chart 2	Tim, miss, pin, in, assistant
Chart 3	fist, fit, if, tennis, sniff, did, this, fifth, fifty, thin, independent
Chart 4	lit, until, ill, mill, still, -i-, wit, with, will, swim, wind
Chart 5	sister, strip, kit, kill, kid, kiss, skip, skill, silk, milk, sick
Chart 6	him, his, brick, impossible, -ing, little, give
Chart 8	think, simple, promise, difficult, big
Chart 9	chin, ship, chill, chips, wish, children, Michigan
Chart 10	chicken, criminal, adjective
Chart 11	which, quickly, fantastic, since
Chart 12	physics
Chart 13	finished, vision
Chart 14	list, listen, written
Chart 15	examination
Chart 16	during
Chart 17	zip, dizzy, mission, tissue, schism
Chart 18	pneumatic, million, build, pigeon, different
Chart 19	humanity, mnemonic
Chart 20	medical, medicine, signify, direct, direction, distance, office, official

Spelling: o as in women

Chart 17	women

Spelling: a as in village

Chart 12	courage
Chart 19	language, chocolate

Spelling: **u as in b<u>u</u>sy**
  Chart 12   busy
  Chart 14   business

Spelling: **<u>e</u> as in <u>E</u>nglish**
  Chart 1   puppet
  Chart 3   -ed, independent
  Chart 4   -es
  Chart 7   -e-
  Chart 8   -est
  Chart 10   orchestra
  Chart 11   between
  Chart 12   be-
  Chart 13   England
  Chart 14   business, knowledge
  Chart 15   believe, receipt, exaggerate, examination
  Chart 17   women
  Chart 18   budget
  Chart 19   except, exhibit, mnemonic
  Chart 20   exhaust

Spelling: **i<u>a</u> as in marr<u>ia</u>ge**
  Chart   No words on the charts

Spelling: **i<u>e</u> as in s<u>ie</u>ve**
  Chart 15   sieve
  Chart 19   handkerchief

Spelling: **<u>ae</u> as in c<u>ae</u>sarian**
  Chart   No words on the charts

Spelling: <u>y</u> as in g<u>y</u>m

Chart 10   gym
Chart 12   physics
Chart 17   rhythm
Chart 19   hymn

Spelling: <u>ee</u> as in b<u>ee</u>n

Chart 6   been

Spelling: <u>ai</u> as in portr<u>ai</u>t

Chart   No words on the charts

Spelling: <u>ei</u> as in forf<u>ei</u>t

Chart   No words on the charts

Spelling: <u>hi</u> as in ex<u>hi</u>bit

Chart 19   exhibit

Spelling: <u>hea</u> as in for<u>hea</u>d

Chart   No words on the charts

4 ice blue: e as in p<u>e</u>t

Spelling: <u>e</u> as in p<u>e</u>t

Chart 1	pet, pep, set, step, steps, pest, Tess, tests, asset
Chart 2	met, mess, net, ten, men, tent, spent, sent, tempt, attempt
Chart 3	tennis, mend, end, fed, them, then, yes, yet, independent
Chart 4	let, sell, tell, less, spell, lend, lent, slept, wet, well, went, sunset, else
Chart 5	red, rest, neck, dress
Chart 7	seven, egg, get, leg
Chart 9	shell, every, ever
Chart 10	shred, schedule, next, education, generation
Chart 11	question
Chart 12	elephant, better
Chart 14	lesson
Chart 16	help
Chart 17	Wednesday
Chart 18	venture, pension, special
Chart 19	except, accept, length, conscientious, shepherd, finesse
Chart 20	guest, debt, medical, medicine, precious, cassette, direct, direction

Spelling: <u>ea</u> as in h<u>ea</u>d

Chart 15	read, meant, treasure

Spelling: <u>a</u> as in <u>a</u>ny

Chart 5	any

Spelling: <u>u</u> as in b<u>u</u>ry
Chart 20   bury

Spelling: <u>ai</u> as in s<u>ai</u>d
Chart 14   said, again

Spelling: <u>ay</u> as in s<u>ay</u>s
Chart 13   says

Spelling: <u>ie</u> as in fr<u>ie</u>nd
Chart 15   friend

Spelling: <u>eo</u> as in l<u>eo</u>pard
Chart 19   leopard

Spelling: <u>ei</u> as in h<u>ei</u>fer
Chart 19   heifer

Spelling: <u>ae</u> as in <u>ae</u>sthetic
Chart   No words on the charts

5   white: o as in pot

Spelling: o as in pot

Chart 1	pot, pop, tot, top, stop, spot, stops
Chart 2	Tom, mom, mops, not, on
Chart 4	doll, lot
Chart 6	hot, impossible, sorry
Chart 7	got
Chart 8	promise
Chart 9	shop, shock
Chart 10	box, job
Chart 13	stopped
Chart 16	clock
Chart 19	conscientious, chocolate, mnemonic

Spelling: a as in swap

Chart 9	watch
Chart 11	what

Spelling: ho as in honor

Chart	No words on the charts

Spelling: oh as in John

Chart	No words on the charts

Spelling: ow as in knowledge

Chart 14	knowledge

Spelling: <u>eau</u> as in bur<u>eau</u>cracy

Chart   No words on the charts

6 yellow: u<u>a</u>ble (the schwa)

Spelling: <u>a</u> as in us<u>a</u>ble

Chart 2	a, attempt, assistant
Chart 7	fatal
Chart 9	China, Michigan
Chart 10	criminal, orchestra, character
Chart 11	capable
Chart 12	elephant, about, sugar
Chart 13	above, England
Chart 14	again
Chart 15	theater
Chart 17	woman, diaphragm
Chart 18	awkward, amoeba, aerial, equals
Chart 19	garage, appreciate, machine
Chart 20	guarantee, medical, acquire, blackguard, asthma, cassette, distance

Spelling: <u>u</u> as in <u>u</u>pon

Chart 4	until
Chart 8	difficult
Chart 9	chorus
Chart 10	schedule, education
Chart 13	Saturday
Chart 15	treasure
Chart 16	autumn
Chart 18	venture
Chart 20	azure

Spelling: <u>i</u> as in poss<u>i</u>ble

Chart 6	impossible
Chart 8	April
Chart 13	family
Chart 19	finesse

Spelling: **io** as in ques**io**n

Chart 10	education
Chart 11	question
Chart 13	vision
Chart 15	examination
Chart 17	mission
Chart 18	pension
Chart 20	direction

Spelling: **iou** as in anx**iou**s

Chart 15	anxious
Chart 19	conscientious
Chart 20	precious

Spelling: **eou** as in right**eou**s

Chart	No words on the charts

Spelling: **ia** as in mart**ia**l

Chart 18	special, spatial
Chart 19	Asia
Chart 20	official

Spelling: **ie** as in consc**ie**nce

Chart 10	soldier
Chart 20	ancient

Spelling:	<u>au</u> as in rest<u>au</u>rant
Chart	No words on the charts

Spelling:	<u>ea</u> as in pag<u>ea</u>nt
Chart 15	ocean

Spelling:	<u>ah</u> as in halleluj<u>ah</u>
Chart 18	hallelujah

Spelling:	ve<u>he</u>ment
Chart	No words on the charts

Spelling:	<u>e</u> as in th<u>e</u>
Chart 3	the, independent
Chart 5	after, sister
Chart 6	father, mother, brother
Chart 7	seven, refuse, united
Chart 8	hundred, -er, open
Chart 9	channel, children, ever, even
Chart 10	chicken, neither, character
Chart 11	garden, quiet
Chart 12	elephant, shoulder, better
Chart 13	under, received
Chart 14	listen, fasten, written, -tieth
Chart 15	theater, anxiety, exaggerate
Chart 16	daughter, water
Chart 17	number, flowers
Chart 18	hallelujah, jewel, often, different, science
Chart 19	handkerchief, heifer, shepherd
Chart 20	stranger, student

Spelling: **o as in conceit**

Chart 3	of
Chart 6	from
Chart 10	potato, tomorrow
Chart 12	photograph
Chart 13	conceit
Chart 14	lesson
Chart 18	champion, mayor
Chart 20	official

Spelling: **ou as in numerous**

| Chart 12 | courageous |
| Chart 20 | luxurious |

Spelling: **oi as in tortoise**

| Chart | No words on the charts |

Spelling: **oa as in cupboard**

| Chart 19 | cupboard |

Spelling: **eo as in pigeon**

| Chart 18 | pigeon |

Spelling: **ai as in captain**

| Chart 20 | certain |

Spelling: **ei as in foreign**

| Chart 19 | foreign |

Spelling:	**iu as in nasturtium**
Chart	No words on the charts

Spelling:	**eau as in bureaucrat**
Chart	No words on the charts

Spelling:	**ough as in thoroughly**
Chart 16	thoroughly

Spelling:	**y as in ethyl**
Chart	No words on the charts

7   blush: u as in fur

Spelling: u as in fur

Chart 5	fur
Chart 7	bursts, hurt
Chart 10	church
Chart 17	Thursday

Spelling: e as in her

Chart 5	were
Chart 6	her
Chart 20	certain

Spelling: o as in work

Chart 5	word, world
Chart 6	work, worry
Chart 12	worse
Chart 16	thoroughly

Spelling: i as in girl

Chart 7	girl, first
Chart 8	dirty, thirty, thirsty

Spelling: ea as in pearl

Chart 15	heard, pearl

Spelling: <u>ou</u> as in c<u>ou</u>rtesy
Chart 12   courage

Spelling: <u>y</u> as in m<u>y</u>rrh
Chart   No words on the charts

8 ochre: o as in off

Spelling: **o as in off**

Chart 8	gone, off, dog, lost
Chart 10	tomorrow
Chart 14	wrong
Chart 18	often

Spelling: **a as in all**

Chart 10	small, all, false, call
Chart 12	want

Spelling: **au as in Paul**

Chart 12	cause
Chart 16	autumn

Spelling: **aw as in paw**

Chart 16	saw
Chart 18	awkward

Spelling: **awe as in awe**

Chart 16	awe

Spelling: **ough as in thought**

Chart 16	thought

Spelling: **oa as in broad**

Chart	No words on the charts

Spelling:	**augh** as in d**augh**ter	
Chart 16	daughter, taught	

Spelling:	**oo*** as in fl**oo**r	
Chart 11	door	

Spelling:	**ou** as in c**ou**gh	
Chart 16	cough	

Spelling:	**hau** as in ex**hau**st	
Chart 20	exhaust	

Spelling:	**ho*** as in ex**ho**rt	
Chart	No words on the charts	

Spelling:	**ao*** as in extr**ao**rdinary	
Chart	No words on the charts	

Spelling:	**oi*** as in reserv**oi**r	
Chart	No words on the charts	

Spelling:	**owa*** as in t**owa**rd	
Chart 18	toward	

9 purple: a as in far

Spelling: **a as in far**
- Chart 6 — father
- Chart 9 — far, are, car
- Chart 11 — garden
- Chart 17 — psalm
- Chart 19 — garage
- Chart 20 — argue

Spelling: **ea as in heart**
- Chart 15 — heart

Spelling: **ah as in ah**
- Chart 17 — ah

Spelling: **aa as in bazaar**
- Chart — No words on the charts

Spelling: **au* as in laugh**
- Chart — No words on the charts

Spelling: **e as in sergeant**
- Chart — No words on the charts

Spelling: **oi as in reservoir**
- Chart — No words on the charts

10 dark green: <u>o</u> as in d<u>o</u>

Spelling: <u>o</u> as in d<u>o</u>

    Chart 6   do, to, move
    Chart 11   whom, who, whose

Spelling: <u>oo</u> as in t<u>oo</u>

    Chart 6   too, zoo, food
    Chart 10   school
    Chart 12   tooth

Spelling: <u>ew</u> as in n<u>ew</u>

    Chart 14   news, new, knew
    Chart 18   jewel

Spelling: <u>ou</u> as in s<u>ou</u>p

    Chart 11   you
    Chart 12   soup

Spelling: <u>ui</u> as in fr<u>ui</u>t

    Chart 16   fruit, suit

Spelling: <u>u</u> as in fl<u>u</u>

    Chart 18   hallelujah
    Chart 20   student

Spelling: <u>oe</u> as in sh<u>oe</u>
Chart 18   shoes

Spelling: <u>ue</u> as in bl<u>ue</u>
Chart 14   true

Spelling: <u>eu</u> as in pn<u>eu</u>matic
Chart 18   pneumatic

Spelling: <u>ough</u> as in thr<u>ough</u>
Chart 16   through

Spelling: <u>wo</u> as in t<u>wo</u>
Chart 6   two

Spelling: <u>ieu</u> as in l<u>ieu</u>tenant
Chart   No words on the charts

11 red: <u>e</u> as in w<u>e</u>

Spelling: <u>e</u> as in w<u>e</u>

Chart 3	fifty
Chart 7	be, we, me, he, the, here
Chart 9	she, even
Chart 11	these
Chart 15	theater, create
Chart 18	equals
Chart 19	appreciate

Spelling: <u>ee</u> as in s<u>ee</u>

Chart 11	seen, see, sleep, feet, between
Chart 12	teeth
Chart 14	eighteen, knee
Chart 16	sweet
Chart 20	guarantee

Spelling: <u>ea</u> as in t<u>ea</u>

Chart 9	teach
Chart 15	ear, hear, tear, read, eat, please, means

Spelling: <u>y</u> as in fift<u>y</u>

Chart 3	-y, fifty
Chart 4	tummy, daddy, funny
Chart 5	any, -ly
Chart 6	sorry, worry
Chart 8	hungry, dirty, thirty, thirsty
Chart 9	very, every
Chart 11	quickly
Chart 12	busy
Chart 13	family

Chart 14	eighty
Chart 15	anxiety
Chart 16	thoroughly
Chart 17	dizzy
Chart 19	humanity, beauty
Chart 20	bury

Spelling: <u>ie</u> as in f<u>ie</u>ld

Chart 13	field
Chart 15	believe

Spelling: <u>ei</u> as in conc<u>ei</u>t

Chart 10	neither
Chart 13	conceit, received
Chart 15	receipt, seize

Spelling: <u>i</u> as in sk<u>i</u>

Chart 14	-tieth
Chart 16	suite
Chart 17	khaki
Chart 18	champion, aerial
Chart 19	appreciate, conscientious, machine
Chart 20	luxurious

Spelling: <u>eo</u> as in p<u>eo</u>ple

Chart	No words on the charts

Spelling: <u>ey</u> as in k<u>ey</u>

Chart 13	money, honey
Chart 17	key

Spelling: <u>ay</u> as in qu<u>ay</u>
Chart 13   Saturday
Chart 17   Thursday, Wednesday, quay

Spelling: <u>oe</u> as in am<u>oe</u>ba
Chart 18   amoeba

Spelling: <u>ae</u> as in <u>ae</u>gis
Chart   No words on the charts

Spelling: <u>is</u> as in debr<u>is</u>
Chart   No words on the charts

Spelling: <u>ois</u> as in cham<u>ois</u>
Chart   No words on the charts

12 turquoise: a as in care

Spelling: a as in care
Chart 9   share

Spelling: ai as in air
Chart 9   hair, air, pair

Spelling: ea as in pear
Chart 15   pear, tear

Spelling: e as in there
Chart 6   there
Chart 11   where

Spelling: ei as in their
Chart 15   their

Spelling: hei as in heir
Chart 14   heir

Spelling: ae as in aerial
Chart 18   aerial

Spelling: <u>aye</u> as in pr<u>aye</u>rs
Chart 13   prayers

Spelling: <u>ayo</u>* as in m<u>ayo</u>r
Chart   No words on the charts

Spelling: <u>ey</u> as in th<u>ey</u>'re
Chart   No words on the charts

13 mouse: oo as in look

Spelling: oo as in look

Chart 6	took, look
Chart 11	foot
Chart 16	poor

Spelling: ou as in would

Chart 11	your
Chart 12	could, should, would, wood, good

Spelling: u as in put

Chart 6	full, put
Chart 9	push
Chart 12	sugar, sure
Chart 20	luxurious

Spelling: o as in woman

Chart 17	woman

14 pink / mouse: u as in cure

Spelling: u as in cure
Chart 15   during, pure

Spelling: eu as in Europe
Chart   No words on the charts

15 brown: o as in or

Spelling: **o as in or**

Chart 7	more, for, or, nor, horse
Chart 8	gone, off, dog, lost
Chart 10	tomorrow, orchestra
Chart 12	fore
Chart 13	talk, walk
Chart 14	wrong, sword, sworn
Chart 16	sore, bored
Chart 18	often
Chart 19	foreign
Chart 20	office, exhaust

Spelling: **a as in war**

Chart	No words on the charts

Spelling: **au as in dinosaur**

Chart	No words on the charts

Spelling: **oa as in board**

Chart 16	soar, board

Spelling: **oo as in door**

Chart 11	door

Spelling: <u>ou</u> as in p<u>ou</u>r
Chart 12   four

Spelling: <u>ho</u> as in ex<u>h</u>ort
Chart   No words on the charts

Spelling: <u>ao</u> as in extr<u>ao</u>rdinary
Chart   No words on the charts

Spelling: <u>oi</u>* as in reserv<u>oi</u>r
Chart   No words on the charts

Spelling: <u>owa</u> as in t<u>owa</u>rd
Chart 18   toward

16 white / pink: I as in I

Spelling: <u>I</u> as in <u>I</u>
- Chart 2 — I

Spelling: <u>i</u> as in l<u>i</u>ke
- Chart 4 — wind
- Chart 5 — mind, wild, mine, strike, find, time, mile, like
- Chart 6 — five
- Chart 7 — iron, united
- Chart 9 — China, child
- Chart 10 — crime
- Chart 11 — quiet, while
- Chart 12 — side, hind
- Chart 14 — write
- Chart 15 — anxiety
- Chart 17 — diaphragm, sign
- Chart 18 — life, science
- Chart 19 — sapphire
- Chart 20 — choir, acquire

Spelling: <u>y</u> as in m<u>y</u>
- Chart 5 — my
- Chart 6 — by
- Chart 10 — cry
- Chart 11 — why
- Chart 14 — buy
- Chart 17 — rhyme
- Chart 20 — signify

Spelling: <u>ie</u> as in l<u>ie</u>
Chart 13   lie

Spelling: <u>ye</u> as in d<u>ye</u>
Chart 14   dye

Spelling: <u>igh</u> as in h<u>igh</u>
Chart 13   high, night, might
Chart 14   fright, right

Spelling: <u>eye</u> as in <u>eye</u>s
Chart 13   eyes

Spelling: <u>eigh</u> as in h<u>eigh</u>t
Chart 13   height

Spelling: <u>is</u> as in <u>is</u>le
Chart 17   isle

Spelling: <u>ais</u> as in <u>ais</u>le
Chart 17   aisle

Spelling: <u>ei</u>* as in <u>ei</u>ther
Chart   No words on the charts

Spelling: <u>aye</u> as in <u>aye</u>

Chart   No words on the charts

17 ice blue / pink: a as in late

Spelling: **a as in late**

Chart 7	hate, date, late, male, take, same, made, fatal
Chart 8	April, able
Chart 10	education, generation, potato, ate
Chart 11	phrase, capable,
Chart 12	courageous, age
Chart 15	create, exaggerate, examination
Chart 17	ache
Chart 18	bathe, spatial
Chart 19	appreciate, Asia
Chart 20	stranger, ancient

Spelling: **ai as in mail**

Chart 13	paid, mail,

Spelling: **ay as in day**

Chart 13	may, way, day, say
Chart 18	mayor

Spelling: **ey as in they**

Chart 13	they, greyhound

Spelling: **ei as in vein**

Chart 15	vein

Spelling:	**eigh** as in **eigh**t
Chart 14	eighth, eighteen, eighty, freight

Spelling:	**ea** as in gr**ea**t
Chart 15	great, break

Spelling:	**aigh** as in str**aigh**t
Chart 18	straight

Spelling:	**et** as in ball**et**
Chart 19	ballet

Spelling:	**ae** as in Isr**ae**li
Chart	No words on the charts

Spelling:	**au** as in g**au**ge
Chart 15	gauge

Spelling:	**e** as in su**e**de
Chart	No words on the charts

Spelling:	**ee** as in fianc**ee**
Chart	No words on the charts

18 brown / aqua: o as in go

Spelling: **o as in go**

Chart 6	won't, don't
Chart 7	bone, woke, nose, home, no, go, so, globe
Chart 8	both, sold, told, cold, hope, most, open
Chart 9	close
Chart 10	soldier, potato
Chart 11	those
Chart 12	photograph
Chart 13	rolled
Chart 15	ocean
Chart 16	broke
Chart 17	zero, ghost
Chart 18	clothes
Chart 20	rogue

Spelling: **oe as in goes**

Chart 8	goes

Spelling: **ow as in know**

Chart 10	tomorrow
Chart 12	low
Chart 14	know
Chart 16	sow
Chart 17	flown

Spelling: **owe as in owe**

Chart	No words on the charts

Spelling: <u>oa</u> as in j<u>oa</u>n
Chart 16   cloak
Chart 17   loaves, loaf

Spelling: <u>ou</u> as in s<u>ou</u>l
Chart 12   shoulder
Chart 14   soul

Spelling: <u>ew</u> as in s<u>ew</u>
Chart 16   sew

Spelling: <u>oh</u> as in <u>oh</u>
Chart 16   oh

Spelling: <u>ough</u> as in th<u>ough</u>
Chart 16   though

Spelling: <u>eau</u> as in plat<u>eau</u>
Chart   No words on the charts

Spelling: <u>oo</u> as in br<u>oo</u>ch
Chart   No words on the charts

Spelling: <u>au</u> as in m<u>au</u>ve
Chart   No words on the charts

Spelling: <u>eo</u> as in y<u>eo</u>man

Chart   No words on the charts

Spelling: <u>ot</u> as in dep<u>ot</u>

Chart   No words on the charts

19 pink / dark green: u as in use

Spelling: u as in use

Chart 7 use, refuse, united, cute
Chart 19 humanity

Spelling: ew as in few

Chart 14 few

Spelling: iew as in view

Chart 18 view

Spelling: eau as in beauty

Chart 19 beauty

Spelling: ue as in hue

Chart 17 tissue
Chart 20 argue

Spelling: ieu as in adieu

Chart No words on the charts

Spelling: ewe as in ewe

Chart No words on the charts

Spelling: <u>hu</u> as in ex<u>hu</u>me

Chart   No words on the charts

Spelling: <u>eu</u> as in f<u>eu</u>dal

Chart   No words on the charts

Spelling: <u>eue</u> as in qu<u>eue</u>

Chart 18   queue

20 purple / aqua: <u>ou</u> as in h<u>ou</u>se

Spelling: <u>ou</u> as in h<u>ou</u>se

- Chart 11 — mouth
- Chart 12 — out, our, house, about
- Chart 13 — greyhound
- Chart 16 — doubt

Spelling: <u>hou</u> as in <u>hou</u>r

- Chart 12 — hour

Spelling: <u>ow</u> as in h<u>ow</u>

- Chart 12 — how, now
- Chart 13 — down
- Chart 16 — sow
- Chart 17 — flowers

Spelling: <u>ough</u> as in b<u>ough</u>

- Chart 16 — bough

21 ochre / pink: <u>oi</u> as in <u>oi</u>l

Spelling: <u>oi</u> as in <u>oi</u>l
Chart 17   oil

Spelling: <u>oy</u> as in b<u>oy</u>
Chart 17   boy, buoy

Spelling: <u>aw</u>* as in l<u>aw</u>yer
Chart   No words on the charts

22 aqua / purple: <u>oi</u> as in reserv<u>oi</u>r

Spelling: <u>oi</u> as in reserv<u>oi</u>r
Chart   No words on the charts

23 aqua / pale yellow: <u>o</u> as in <u>o</u>ne

Spelling: <u>o</u> as in <u>o</u>ne
Chart 11   once, one

Consonant Sounds & Spellings

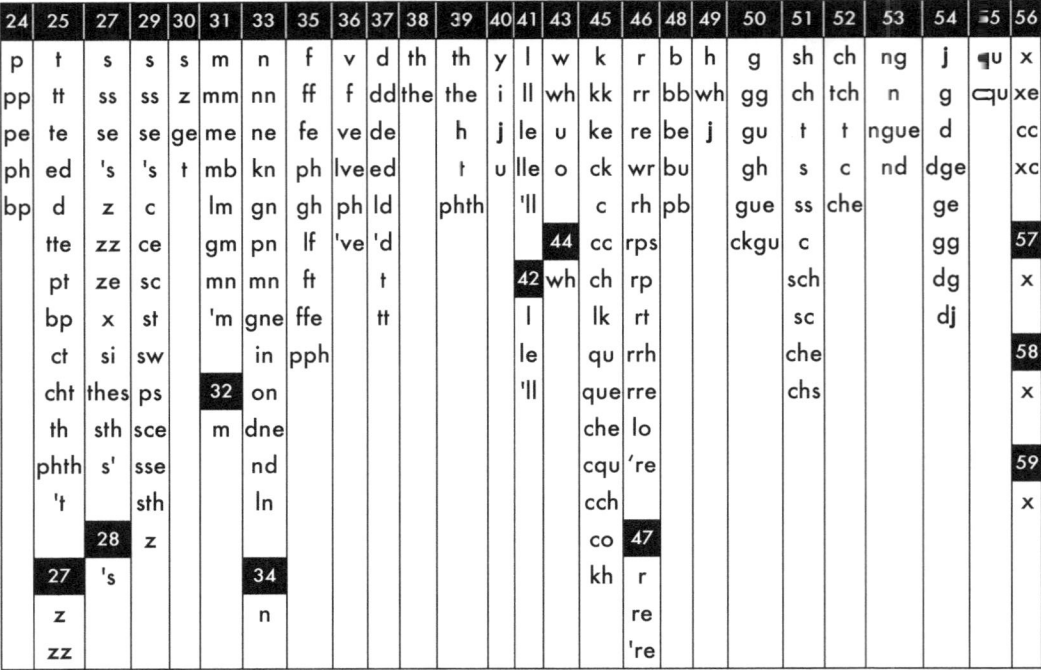

24 chestnut: p as in p<u>o</u>t

Spelling: <u>p</u> as in <u>p</u>ot

- Chart 1 — pat, pit, pet, pot, pop, up, putt, top, tip, tap, apt, pep, pup, sap, stop, step, spot, stops, steps, pass, pest, sips, past, puppet
- Chart 2 — mumps, mops, pump, stamps, map, Pam, spent, pants, pin, tempt, attempt
- Chart 3 — puff, independent, path
- Chart 4 — spell, lap, pal, plus, slept
- Chart 5 — strip, skip
- Chart 6 — impossible, put
- Chart 8 — bankrupt, April, simple, promise, open
- Chart 9 — shop, ship, chips, push, pair
- Chart 10 — potato
- Chart 11 — capable, sleep
- Chart 12 — soup
- Chart 13 — paid, prayers
- Chart 15 — please, pear, pearl
- Chart 16 — pure, poor, help
- Chart 17 — zip
- Chart 18 — champion, pension, pigeon, special, spatial
- Chart 19 — except, accept, plaque, leopard
- Chart 20 — precious

Spelling: <u>pp</u> as in sto<u>pp</u>ed

- Chart 1 — puppet
- Chart 13 — stopped
- Chart 19 — appreciate

Spelling: **pe** as in ho**pe**
Chart 8   hope

Spelling: **ph** as in she**ph**erd
Chart 19   shepherd

Spelling: **bp** as in su**bp**oena
Chart   No words on the charts

25 fuchsia: t as in top

Spelling: t as in top

Chart 1	pat, pit, pet, pot, at, it, tot, top, tip, tap, apt, sat, set, stop, step, spot, stops, steps, pest, Tess, tests, past, puppet, asset
Chart 2	mat, Tim, met, Tom, must, mast, stamps, not, nut, net, ten, tent, spent, sent, pants, tempt, attempt, assistant
Chart 3	fist, fit, fat, stuff, dust, tennis, stand, that, fifty, yet, independent
Chart 4	let, tell, lit, lot, lent, until, still, last, slept, tummy, wit, wet, went, sunset
Chart 5	rat, after, rust, sister, rest, strip, kit, strike, time
Chart 6	hot, hat, to, two, too, took, put, but
Chart 7	take, fatal, united, bursts, hurt, first, got, get
Chart 8	bankrupt, told, dirty, thirty, thirsty, -est, lost, difficult, most
Chart 9	shut, teach, front
Chart 10	adjective, next, act, potato, tomorrow, orchestra, character
Chart 11	quiet, fantastic, foot, feet, between, what
Chart 12	elephant, photograph, out, tooth, about, teeth, want
Chart 13	height, night, Saturday, might, stopped, conceit, talk
Chart 14	eighth, eighteen, eighty, freight, fright, list, fast, right, -tieth
Chart 15	tear, theater, heart, eat, meant, great, tear, anxiety
Chart 16	autumn, daughter, taught, water, tough, thought, sweet, fruit, suit
Chart 17	ghost, tissue, waltz
Chart 18	pneumatic, toward, different, budget, straight
Chart 19	except, exhibit, accept, humanity, beauty
Chart 20	guest, guarantee, tongue, stranger, ancient, certain, student, direct, distance, exhaust

Spelling: <u>tt</u> as in li<u>tt</u>le

Chart 1	putt,
Chart 2	attempt
Chart 6	little
Chart 12	better
Chart 14	written

Spelling: <u>te</u> as in la<u>te</u>

Chart 7	hate, date, late, cute
Chart 10	ate
Chart 14	write
Chart 15	create, exaggerate
Chart 16	suite
Chart 19	appreciate, chocolate

Spelling: <u>ed</u> as in finish<u>ed</u>

Chart 3	-ed
Chart 13	finished, stopped

Spelling: <u>d</u> as in place<u>d</u>

Chart	No words on the charts

Spelling: <u>tte</u> as in casse<u>tte</u>

Chart 20	cassette

Spelling: <u>pt</u> as in recei<u>pt</u>

Chart 15	receipt

Spelling: <u>bt</u> as in de<u>bt</u>
   Chart 16   doubt
   Chart 20   debt

Spelling: <u>ct</u> as in indi<u>ct</u>
   Chart   No words on the charts

Spelling: <u>cht</u> as in ya<u>cht</u>
   Chart   No words on the charts

Spelling: <u>th</u> as in <u>th</u>yme
   Chart   No words on the charts

Spelling: <u>phth</u> as in <u>phth</u>isic
   Chart   No words on the charts

Spelling: '<u>t</u> as in don'<u>t</u>
   Chart 6   -n't, won't, don't

26 fuchsia / lime green: <u>z</u> as in schi<u>z</u>o

Spelling: <u>z</u> as in schi<u>z</u>ophrenic
   Chart   No words on the charts

Spelling: <u>zz</u> as in pi<u>zz</u>a
   Chart   No words on the charts

27 lilac: s as in is

Spelling: **s as in is**

Chart 1	as, is, -s, 's
Chart 4	-es, was
Chart 6	has, his
Chart 8	goes, does
Chart 12	physics, busy
Chart 13	eyes, prayers, says
Chart 14	news
Chart 15	means
Chart 17	loaves, calves, flowers, Thursday, Wednesday, schism
Chart 18	shoes, equals

Spelling: **ss as in scissors**

Chart	No words on the charts

Spelling: **se as in hose**

Chart 7	nose, refuse
Chart 11	phrase, these, those, whose
Chart 12	cause
Chart 15	please

Spelling: **s as in Pam's**

Chart 1	's

Spelling: <u>z</u> as in <u>z</u>oo
Chart 6   zoo
Chart 17 zero, zip

Spelling: <u>zz</u> as in di<u>zz</u>y
Chart 17 dizzy

Spelling: <u>ze</u> as in sei<u>ze</u>
Chart 15 seize

Spelling: <u>x</u> as in an<u>x</u>iety
Chart 15 anxiety

Spelling: <u>si</u> as in bu<u>si</u>ness
Chart 14 business

Spelling: <u>thes</u> as in clo<u>thes</u>
Chart 18 clothes

Spelling: <u>sth</u> as in a<u>sth</u>ma
Chart 20 asthma

Spelling: <u>s'</u> as in boy<u>s'</u>
Chart   No words on the charts

28 yellow / lilac: '<u>s</u> as in James'<u>s</u>

Spelling: '<u>s</u> as in James'<u>s</u>

Chart   No words on the charts

29 lime green: s as in us

Spelling: s as in us

Chart 1	us, sat, sit, set, sap, -s, stop, step, spot, stops, steps, pest, sips, tests, past
Chart 2	must, mumps, mast, mops, stamps, sum, Sam, spent, sent, pants, sun, son, assistant
Chart 3	fist, stuff, dust, tennis, sniff, sad, stand, this, sand, yes
Chart 4	sell, spell, still, last, plus, slept, swim, sunset
Chart 5	rust, sister, rest, strip, ask, skip, skill, silk, sick, strike
Chart 6	sorry
Chart 7	same, seven, so, bursts, first
Chart 8	sold, some, thirsty, -est, simple, lost, most
Chart 9	chips, such, chorus
Chart 10	small, school, schedule, soldier, orchestra
Chart 11	question, seen, fantastic, see, sleep, since
Chart 12	physics, soup, courageous, side
Chart 13	Saturday, stopped, says, say
Chart 14	list, fast, sworn, said, soul
Chart 15	sieve, seize, anxious
Chart 16	saw, sore, soar, sew, sow, sow, sweet, suit, suite
Chart 17	ghost, sign, schism
Chart 18	special, spatial, straight
Chart 19	conscientious, sapphire
Chart 20	guest, stranger, signify, precious, luxurious, student, distance, exhaust

Spelling: **ss as in pass**

Chart 1	pass, Tess, asset
Chart 2	miss, mess, assistant
Chart 4	less
Chart 5	kiss, dress
Chart 6	impossible
Chart 14	lesson, business
Chart 20	cassette

Spelling: **se as in promise**

Chart 4	else
Chart 7	horse, use
Chart 8	promise
Chart 9	close
Chart 10	false
Chart 12	house, worse

Spelling: **'s as in pat's**

| Chart 1 | 's |

Spelling: **c as in receipt**

Chart 13	conceit, received
Chart 15	receipt
Chart 20	medicine, certain

Spelling: **ce as in once**

Chart 11	once, since
Chart 18	science
Chart 20	distance, office

Spelling:	**sc** as in **sc**ience
Chart 18	science

Spelling:	**st** as in li**st**en
Chart 14	listen, fasten

Spelling:	**sw** as in **sw**ord
Chart 14	sword

Spelling:	**ps** as in **ps**ychology
Chart 17	psalm

Spelling:	**sce** as in acquie**sce**
Chart	No words on the charts

Spelling:	**sse** as in fine**sse**
Chart 19	finesse

Spelling:	**sth** as in i**sth**mus
Chart	No words on the charts

Spelling:	**z** as in wal**tz**
Chart 17	waltz

30 French blue: <u>s</u> as in mea<u>s</u>ure

Spelling: <u>s</u> as in mea<u>s</u>ure
   Chart 13   vision
   Chart 15   treasure
   Chart 19   Asia

Spelling: <u>z</u> as in a<u>z</u>ure
   Chart 20   azure

Spelling: <u>ge</u> as in <u>g</u>ara<u>ge</u>
   Chart 19   garage

Spelling: <u>t</u> as in equa<u>t</u>ion
   Chart   No words on the charts

31 orange: <u>m</u> as in <u>m</u>at

Spelling: <u>m</u> as in <u>m</u>at

Chart 2	mat, Tim, met, Tom, mom, must, mumps, mast, mops, miss, mess, pump, am, stamps, map, sum, Sam, Pam, man, men, tempt, attempt
Chart 3	mad, mend, mud, them, yam
Chart 4	mill, swim
Chart 5	my, mind, mine, milk, mile
Chart 6	him, impossible, mother, move, from
Chart 7	male, more, made, me
Chart 8	month, simple, promise, most
Chart 9	match, much, Michigan
Chart 10	small, gym, criminal, tomorrow
Chart 11	mouth, whom
Chart 13	might, money, mail, may, family
Chart 15	meant, means, examination
Chart 17	number, woman, women, mission
Chart 18	pneumatic, champion, million, amoeba, mayor
Chart 19	humanity, mnemonic, machine
Chart 20	medical, medicine, asthma

Spelling: <u>mm</u> as in co<u>mm</u>a

Chart 4	tummy

Spelling: <u>me</u> as in sa<u>me</u>

Chart 5	time
Chart 7	same, home
Chart 8	come, some
Chart 10	crime
Chart 17	rhyme

Spelling: <u>mb</u> as in la<u>mb</u>
Chart 14   dumb

Spelling: <u>lm</u> as in ca<u>lm</u>
Chart 17   psalm

Spelling: <u>gm</u> as in diaphra<u>gm</u>
Chart 17   diaphragm

Spelling: <u>mn</u> as in hy<u>mn</u>
Chart 16   autumn
Chart 19   hymn

Spelling: <u>'m</u> as in I<u>'m</u>
Chart 2   'm

32 yellow / orange: <u>m</u> as in rhyth<u>m</u>

Spelling: <u>m</u> as in rhyth<u>m</u>
Chart 17   rhythm, schism

33 lavender: n as in pin

Spelling: **n as in pin**

Chart 2	not, nut, net, ten, man, men, tent, spent, sent, pants, pin, sun, an, in, on, son, assistant
Chart 3	fan, fun, and, sniff, mend, stand, end, sand, then, than, thin, independent
Chart 4	land, lend, lent, until, went, wind, sunset, wind
Chart 5	ran, run, mind, any, neck, find
Chart 6	been, won't, don't
Chart 7	nor, nose, seven, no, united
Chart 8	month, hundred, hand, open
Chart 9	chin, China, front, children, Michigan, even
Chart 10	chicken, criminal, neither, next, education, generation
Chart 11	garden, question, seen, once, fantastic, between, when, since
Chart 12	elephant, now, gun, hind, want
Chart 13	night, under, money, down, honey, finished, conceit, vision, greyhound, England
Chart 14	eighteen, listen, news, fasten, lesson, business, sworn, new, again, written
Chart 15	friend, meant, vein, ocean, means, examination
Chart 17	number, flown, woman, women, mission
Chart 18	champion, venture, million, pension, often, pigeon, different, science
Chart 19	conscientious, humanity, mnemonic, finesse
Chart 20	guarantee, stranger, signify, ancient, certain, student, direction, distance

Spelling: **nn as in funny**

Chart 3	tennis
Chart 4	funny
Chart 9	channel

Spelling: <u>ne</u> as in fi<u>ne</u>

Chart 5	mine
Chart 7	bone
Chart 8	done, gone
Chart 11	one
Chart 19	machine
Chart 20	medicine

Spelling: <u>kn</u> as in <u>kn</u>ow

Chart 14	know, knee, knew, knowledge

Spelling: <u>gn</u> as in si<u>gn</u>

Chart 17	sign
Chart 19	foreign

Spelling: <u>pn</u> as in <u>pn</u>eumatic

Chart 18	pneumatic

Spelling: <u>mn</u> as in <u>mn</u>emonic

Chart 19	mnemonic

Spelling: <u>gne</u> as in champa<u>gne</u>

Chart	No words on the charts

Spelling: <u>in</u> as in extraord<u>in</u>ary

Chart	No words on the charts

Spelling:	<u>on</u> as in ir<u>on</u>	
Chart 7	iron	

Spelling:	<u>dne</u> as in We<u>dne</u>sday	
Chart 17	Wednesday	

Spelling:	<u>nd</u> as in gra<u>nd</u>father	
Chart	No words on the charts	

Spelling:	<u>ln</u> as in Linco<u>ln</u>	
Chart	No words on the charts	

34 yellow / lavender: <u>n</u> as in would<u>n</u>'t

Spelling:	<u>n</u> as in would<u>n</u>'t	
Chart 6	-n't	

35 mauve: f as in if

Spelling: **f as in if**

Chart 3	fan, fun, fist, fit, if, fat, fed, fifth, fifty
Chart 4	funny
Chart 5	after, find, fur
Chart 6	father, food, full, five, from
Chart 7	for, fatal, refuse, first
Chart 9	front, far
Chart 10	false
Chart 11	fantastic, foot, feet
Chart 12	four, fore
Chart 13	finished, field, family
Chart 14	freight, fright, few, fast, fasten
Chart 15	friend
Chart 16	fruit
Chart 17	loaf, flown, flowers
Chart 19	handkerchief, foreign, heifer, finesse
Chart 20	signify

Spelling: **ff as in off**

Chart 3	stuff, puff, sniff
Chart 8	off, difficult
Chart 20	office, official

Spelling: **fe as in life**

Chart 18	life

Spelling: **ph as in photograph**
- Chart 11 phrase
- Chart 12 physics, elephant, photograph
- Chart 17 diaphragm

Spelling: **gh as in cough**
- Chart 16 tough, laugh, cough

Spelling: **lf as in half**
- Chart 17 half

Spelling: **ft as in often**
- Chart 18 often

Spelling: **ffe as in giraffe**
- Chart 18 different

Spelling: **pph as in sapphire**
- Chart 19 sapphire

36 khaki: <u>v</u> as in se<u>v</u>en

Spelling: <u>v</u> as in se<u>v</u>en

    Chart 7   seven
    Chart 9   very, every, ever, even
    Chart 13   vision
    Chart 15   vein
    Chart 18   venture, view

Spelling: <u>f</u> as in o<u>f</u>

    Chart 3   of

Spelling: <u>ve</u> as in gi<u>ve</u>

    Chart 5   love
    Chart 6   have, move, five, give
    Chart 10   adjective
    Chart 13   above, received
    Chart 15   believe, sieve
    Chart 17   loaves

Spelling: <u>lve</u> as in ha<u>lve</u>s

    Chart 17   calves

Spelling: <u>ph</u> as in Ste<u>ph</u>en

    Chart   No words on the charts

Spelling: 've as in I've

Chart 6   've

37 green: <u>d</u> as in <u>d</u>ust

Spelling: <u>d</u> as in <u>d</u>ust

Chart 3	dad, mad, and, dud, dust, did, mend, sad, stand, end, -ed, mud, sand, fed, independent
Chart 4	doll, dull, land, lend, daddy, wind, wind
Chart 5	red, mind, wild, kid, dress, find, -d, word, world
Chart 6	do, food, don't
Chart 7	date, united
Chart 8	sold, told, done, cold, hundred, dirty, hand, dog, difficult, does
Chart 9	child, children
Chart 10	shred
Chart 11	garden, blood, door
Chart 12	shoulder, wood, hind
Chart 13	Saturday, under, down, paid, field, day, greyhound, received, England
Chart 14	sword, dumb, said, dye
Chart 15	read, heard, read, friend
Chart 16	during, daughter, doubt, board, bored
Chart 17	dizzy, Thursday, Wednesday, diaphragm
Chart 18	toward, awkward, build, different
Chart 19	cupboard, shepherd, leopard
Chart 20	debt, medical, medicine, blackguard, student, direct, direction, distance

Spelling: <u>dd</u> as in su<u>dd</u>en

Chart 4	add, daddy

Spelling:	**de as in ma<u>de</u>**
Chart 7	made
Chart 12	side

Spelling:	**ed as in roll<u>ed</u>**
Chart 3	-ed
Chart 13	rolled

Spelling:	**ld as in wou<u>ld</u>**
Chart 12	could, should, would

Spelling:	**'d as in I'<u>d</u>**
Chart	No words on the charts

Spelling:	**t* as in wa<u>t</u>er**
Chart	No words on the charts

Spelling:	**tt* as in bu<u>tt</u>er**
Chart	No words on the charts

38 sad pink: <u>th</u> as in <u>th</u>is

Spelling: <u>th</u> as in <u>th</u>is

Chart 3	this, that, them, then, than, the
Chart 4	with
Chart 6	father, mother, brother, there
Chart 7	the
Chart 10	neither
Chart 11	these, those
Chart 13	they
Chart 15	their
Chart 16	though
Chart 17	rhythm

Spelling: <u>the</u> as in ba<u>the</u>

Chart 18	bathe

39 pale lime: <u>th</u> as in <u>th</u>in

Spelling: <u>th</u> as in <u>th</u>in

Chart 3	fif<u>th</u>, <u>th</u>in, pa<u>th</u>
Chart 8	mon<u>th</u>, <u>th</u>ank, <u>th</u>ink, bo<u>th</u>, <u>th</u>irty, <u>th</u>irsty
Chart 11	mou<u>th</u>
Chart 12	too<u>th</u>, tee<u>th</u>
Chart 14	-tie<u>th</u>
Chart 15	<u>th</u>eatre
Chart 16	<u>th</u>ought, <u>th</u>rough, <u>th</u>orough
Chart 17	<u>Th</u>ursday
Chart 19	leng<u>th</u>

Spelling: <u>the</u> as in absin<u>the</u>

Chart — No words on the charts

Spelling: <u>h</u> as in eig<u>h</u>t<u>h</u>

Chart 14 — eighth

Spelling: <u>t</u> as in sou<u>t</u>hampton

Chart — No words on the charts

Spelling: <u>phth</u> as in <u>phth</u>alein

Chart — No words on the charts

40 pink: y as in yes

Spelling: y as in yes

Chart 3   yes, yam, yet
Chart 11   your, you, young

Spelling: i as in onion

Chart 18   million

Spelling: j as in hallelujah

Chart 17   hallelujah

Spelling: u as in vacuum

Chart   No words on the charts

41 bright blue: l as in let

Spelling: l as in let

Chart 4	let, lit, land, less, lot, lap, lend, lent, pal, until, last, plus, slept, else
Chart 5	silk, milk, -ly, like, love, world
Chart 6	black, little, look
Chart 7	late, fatal, girl, globe, leg
Chart 8	sold, told, cold, april, lost, difficult
Chart 9	channel, children, close
Chart 10	school, criminal, false, soldier
Chart 11	quickly, blood, sleep
Chart 12	elephant, low, shoulder
Chart 13	lie, England, family
Chart 14	list, listen, lesson, soul, knowledge
Chart 15	believe, please, pearl
Chart 16	laugh, thoroughly, help, cloak, clock
Chart 17	loaves, loaf, flown, flowers, waltz
Chart 18	hallelujah, life, jewel, clothes, aerial, build, special, spatial, equals
Chart 19	length, language, chocolate, plaque, leopard
Chart 20	medical, blackguard, luxurious, official

Spelling: ll as in sell

Chart 4	doll, dull, sell, tell, spell, ill, mill, still, will, well
Chart 5	kill, skill
Chart 6	full
Chart 9	chill, shell, shall
Chart 10	small, all, call
Chart 13	rolled
Chart 18	hallelujah, million
Chart 19	ballet

Spelling: Chart 10	**le as in pale** schedule
Spelling: Chart	**lle as in gazelle** No words on the charts
Spelling: Chart	**'ll as in he'll** No words on the charts

42 yellow / bright blue: l as in wi_l_d

Spelling: <u>l</u> as in wi<u>l</u>d

- Chart 5 — wild
- Chart 9 — child
- Chart 13 — mail, field
- Chart 17 — oil

Spelling: <u>le</u> as in simp<u>le</u>

- Chart 5 — mile
- Chart 6 — impossible, little
- Chart 7 — male
- Chart 8 — simple, able
- Chart 11 — capable, while
- Chart 17 — isle, aisle

Spelling: '<u>ll</u> as in I'<u>ll</u>

- Chart 4 — 'll

43 pale aqua: <u>w</u> as in <u>w</u>e

Spelling: <u>w</u> as in <u>w</u>et

Chart 4	wit, wet, with, will, swim, was, well, went, w<u>i</u>nd, w<u>i</u>nd
Chart 5	wild, were, word, world
Chart 6	work, worry, won't
Chart 7	we, woke
Chart 9	wish, watch
Chart 11	between
Chart 12	would, worse, wood, want
Chart 13	way, walk
Chart 16	water, sweet
Chart 17	woman, women, wednesday, waltz

Spelling: <u>wh</u> as in <u>wh</u>en

Chart 11	which, while, why, what, where, when

Spelling: <u>u</u> as in s<u>u</u>ite

Chart 16	suite
Chart 19	language

Spelling: <u>o</u> as in ch<u>o</u>ir

Chart 20	choir

44 pale blue / aqua: wh as in where

Spelling: wh* as in where

Chart 11   which, while, why, what, where, when

45 gold: k as in kiss

Spelling: **k as in kiss**

Chart 5	ask, kit, kill, kid, kiss, skip, skill, silk, milk
Chart 6	work, took, look
Chart 8	thank, think, bankrupt
Chart 15	break
Chart 16	cloak
Chart 17	key, khaki
Chart 18	awkward
Chart 19	handkerchief

Spelling: **kk as in trekked**

Chart	No words on the charts

Spelling: **ke as in like**

Chart 5	strike, like
Chart 7	take, woke
Chart 16	broke

Spelling: **ck as in sick**

Chart 5	sick, neck, track, truck
Chart 6	back, brick, black
Chart 9	shock
Chart 10	chicken
Chart 11	quickly
Chart 16	clock

Spelling: <u>c</u> as in <u>c</u>at

Chart 7	cute
Chart 8	come, cold, difficult
Chart 9	cash, close, car
Chart 10	cry, criminal, adjective, call, act, education, crime, character
Chart 11	capable, fantastic
Chart 12	physics, courage, courageous, could, cause
Chart 13	conceit
Chart 15	create
Chart 16	cough, cloak, clock
Chart 18	pneumatic, clothes
Chart 19	conscientious, cupboard, mnemonic
Chart 20	medical, cassette, direct, direction

Spelling: <u>cc</u> as in o<u>cc</u>ur

Chart	No words on the charts

Spelling: <u>ch</u> as in <u>ch</u>orus

Chart 9	chorus
Chart 10	school, schedule, orchestra, character
Chart 17	schism
Chart 20	choir

Spelling: <u>lk</u> as in ta<u>lk</u>

Chart 13	talk, walk

Spelling: <u>qu</u> as in <u>qu</u>ay

Chart 17	quay
Chart 18	queue

Spelling: **que as in clique**
Chart 19   plaque

Spelling: **che as in ache**
Chart 17   ache

Spelling: **cqu as in lacquer**
Chart   No words on the charts

Spelling: **co as in chocolate**
Chart 19   chocolate

Spelling: **kh as in khaki**
Chart 17   khaki

46 light orange: r as in ran

Spelling: r as in ran

Chart 5	ran, rat, after, run, rust, red, sister, rest, strip, track, truck, dress, strike, fur, word, world
Chart 6	her, brick, father, mother, work, brother, from
Chart 7	for, or, nor, horse, refuse, girl, bursts, hurt, first
Chart 8	bankrupt, hungry, hundred, dirty, thirty, thirsty, -er, April, promise
Chart 9	front, children, far, very, car, every, chorus, hair, ever, air, pair
Chart 10	church, cry, shred, criminal, soldier, neither, generation, crime, orchestra, character
Chart 11	phrase, garden, door, your
Chart 12	photograph, courage, four, courageous, shoulder, worse, sugar, better
Chart 13	Saturday, under, prayers, rolled, greyhound, received
Chart 14	freight, fright, heir, sword, sworn, right, true
Chart 15	theater, read, heart, heard, read, friend, receipt, great, pear, create, tear, pearl, their, break, treasure, exaggerate
Chart 16	during, daughter, water, poor, soar, through, thoroughly, board, broke, fruit
Chart 17	number, flowers, zero, Thursday, diaphragm
Chart 18	toward, awkward, aerial, different, mayor, straight
Chart 19	garage, appreciate, handkerchief, cupboard, foreign, heifer, shepherd, leopard
Chart 20	guarantee, bury, stranger, rogue, blackguard, precious, argue, luxurious, certain, direct, direction

Spelling: <u>rr</u> as in ho<u>rr</u>or

Chart 6	sorry, worry
Chart 10	tomorrow

Spelling: <u>re</u> as in mo<u>re</u>

Chart 5	were
Chart 6	there
Chart 7	more
Chart 9	share, are
Chart 11	where
Chart 12	fore, sure
Chart 15	treasure
Chart 16	pure, sore
Chart 18	venture
Chart 20	azure

Spelling: <u>wr</u> as in <u>wr</u>ite

Chart 14	wrong, written, write

Spelling: <u>rh</u> as in <u>r</u>hythm

Chart 17	rhythm, rhyme

Spelling: <u>rps</u> as in co<u>rps</u>

Chart	No words on the charts

Spelling: <u>rp</u> as in co<u>rp</u>sman

Chart	No words on the charts

Spelling: rt as in mortgage
Chart   No words on the charts

Spelling: rrh as in catarrh
Chart   No words on the charts

Spelling: rre as in bizarre
Chart   No words on the charts

Spelling: lo as in colonel
Chart   No words on the charts

Spelling: 're as in you're
Chart   No words on the charts

47 yellow / light orange: r as in iron

Spelling: **r as in iron**
- Chart 7 — iron
- Chart 12 — hour, our
- Chart 15 — ear, hear, tear
- Chart 20 — choir

Spelling: **re as in fire**
- Chart 7 — here
- Chart 19 — sapphire
- Chart 20 — acquire

Spelling: **'re as in we're**
- Chart 7 — 're

48 bottle green: <u>b</u> as in <u>b</u>ay

Spelling: <u>b</u> as in <u>b</u>ay

Chart 6	back, brick, black, impossible, been, by, brother, but
Chart 7	be, bone, bursts
Chart 8	both, bankrupt, able, big
Chart 10	box, job
Chart 11	capable, blood, between
Chart 12	about, be-, busy, better
Chart 13	above
Chart 14	business
Chart 15	believe, break
Chart 16	bough, board, bored, broke
Chart 17	number, boy
Chart 18	bathe, amoeba, budget
Chart 19	exhibit, beauty, ballet
Chart 20	bury, blackguard

Spelling: <u>bb</u> as in ri<u>bb</u>on

Chart	No words on the charts

Spelling: <u>be</u> as in cu<u>be</u>

Chart 7	globe

Spelling: <u>bu</u> as in <u>bu</u>y

Chart 14	buy
Chart 17	buoy
Chart 18	build

Spelling: <u>p</u><u>b</u> as in ras<u>p</u><u>b</u>erry

Chart 19 cupboard

49 pale blue: h as in hat

Spelling: **h as in hat**

Chart 6	hot, has, him, her, his, hat, have
Chart 7	hate, horse, he, here, home, hurt
Chart 8	hungry, hundred, hand, hope
Chart 9	hair
Chart 12	how, house, hind
Chart 13	high, height, honey, greyhound
Chart 15	hear, heart, heard
Chart 16	help
Chart 17	half
Chart 18	hallelujah
Chart 19	handkerchief, humanity, hymn, heifer

Spelling: **wh as in who**

Chart 11	whom, who, whose

Spelling: **j as in jose**

Chart	No words on the charts

50 gray: g as in gray

Spelling: **g as in go**

Chart 6	give
Chart 7	go, girl, got, globe, get, leg
Chart 8	gone, hungry, dog, goes, big
Chart 9	Michigan
Chart 11	garden
Chart 12	photograph, gun, sugar, good
Chart 13	greyhound, England
Chart 14	again
Chart 15	great, gauge
Chart 19	garage, language
Chart 20	signify, argue

Spelling: **gg as in egg**

Chart 7 egg

Spelling: **gu as in guard**

Chart 20 guest, guarantee

Spelling: **gh as in ghost**

Chart 17 ghost

Spelling: **gue as in league**

Chart 20 rogue

Spelling: <u>ckgu</u> as in bla<u>ckgu</u>ard

Chart 20 blackguard

51 sky blue: sh as in she

Spelling: sh as in she

Chart 9	shop, shut, she, ship, wish, push, share, cash, shel , shock, shall
Chart 10	shred
Chart 12	should, shoulder
Chart 13	finished
Chart 18	shoes
Chart 19	shepherd

Spelling: ch as in machine

Chart 9	Michigan
Chart 19	machine

Spelling: t as in education

Chart 10	education, generation
Chart 15	examination
Chart 18	spatial
Chart 19	conscientious
Chart 20	direction

Spelling: s as in sugar

Chart 12	sugar, sure
Chart 18	pension

Spelling: ss as in tissue

Chart 17	mission, tissue

Spelling:	**c** as in appre**c**iate
Chart 15	o**c**ean
Chart 18	spe**c**ial
Chart 19	appre**c**iate
Chart 20	pre**c**ious, an**c**ient, offi**c**ial

Spelling:	**sch** as in **sch**ist
Chart	No words on the charts

Spelling:	**sc** as in con**sc**ience
Chart 19	con**sc**ientious

Spelling:	**che** as in ca**che**
Chart	No words on the charts

Spelling:	**chs** as in fu**chs**ia
Chart	No words on the charts

52 dark magenta: ch as in chin

Spelling: **ch as in chin**

Chart 9	chin, chill, China, teach, chips, much, such, child, channel, children
Chart 10	chicken, church
Chart 11	which
Chart 18	champion
Chart 19	handkerchief, chocolate

Spelling: **tch as in watch**

Chart 9	match, watch

Spelling: **t as in question**

Chart 5	track, truck
Chart 11	question
Chart 14	true
Chart 15	treasure
Chart 18	venture

Spelling: **c as in cello**

Chart	No words on the charts

Spelling: **che as in niche**

Chart	No words on the charts

53 olive: <u>ng</u> as in si<u>ng</u>

Spelling: <u>ng</u> as in si<u>ng</u>

Chart 6	-ing
Chart 11	young
Chart 14	wrong
Chart 16	during
Chart 19	length

Spelling: <u>n</u> as in ba<u>n</u>krupt

Chart 8	thank, think, bankrupt, hungry
Chart 13	England
Chart 15	anxiety, anxious
Chart 19	language

Spelling: <u>ngue</u> as in to<u>ngue</u>

Chart 20	tongue

Spelling: <u>nd</u> as in ha<u>nd</u>kerchief

Chart 19	handkerchief

54 green / French blue: j as in jack

Spelling: j as in jack
- Chart 10 judge, job
- Chart 18 jewel

Spelling: g as in gem
- Chart 10 gym, generation
- Chart 18 pigeon
- Chart 20 stranger

Spelling: d as in soldier
- Chart 10 schedule, soldier, education

Spelling: dge as in judge
- Chart 10 judge
- Chart 14 knowledge

Spelling: ge as in gage
- Chart 12 courage, courageous, age
- Chart 15 gauge
- Chart 19 language

Spelling: gg as in exaggerate
- Chart 15 exaggerate

Spelling: <u>dg</u> as in ju<u>dg</u>ment
Chart 18 budget

Spelling: <u>dj</u> as in a<u>dj</u>ective
Chart 10 adjective

55 gold / aqua: qu as in quickly

Spelling: qu as in quickly
- Chart 11 — question, quiet, quickly
- Chart 18 — equals

Spelling: cqu as in acquiesce
- Chart 20 — acquire

56 gold / lime green: x as in box

Spelling: x as in box
- Chart 10 — box, next

Spelling: xe as in axe
- Chart — No words on the charts

Spelling: cc as in accept
- Chart 19 — accept

Spelling: xc as in excel
- Chart 19 — except

57 gray / lilac: exist

Spelling: x as in exist

- Chart 15   exaggerate, examination
- Chart 19   exhibit
- Chart 20   exhaust

58 gold / sky blue: x as in anxious

Spelling: x as in anxious

- Chart 15   anxious

59 gray / French blue: x as in luxurious

Spelling: x as in luxurious

- Chart 20   luxurious